GALÁPAGOS
ISLANDS OF CHANGE

TEXT BY **LYNNE BORN MYERS** AND **CHRISTOPHER A. MYERS**

GALÁPAGOS
ISLANDS OF CHANGE

PHOTOGRAPHS BY **NATHAN FARB**

HYPERION BOOKS FOR CHILDREN
NEW YORK

T he earth is always undergoing changes. Tides wash away beaches, seas become deserts, mountains rise, some animals go extinct while others come into being, but these changes can take ages to unfold. Only rarely do we catch a glimpse of the remarkable forces that shape life and land.

Perhaps nowhere are the forces of change more evident than in the Galápagos Islands, six hundred miles off the coast of Ecuador in the Pacific Ocean. Change has come to the iguanas that sleep like small dragons on warm lava rocks. It has come to the "vampire" finches that feed on the blood of other birds, and to the mysterious giant tortoises that gather in herds in the craters of old volcanoes. And change rumbles deep below the islands, where the shifting of tremendous heat and pressure within the earth causes the land to tremble and volcanoes to erupt.

This is the story of the Galápagos Islands: of how the islands were born and how they became inhabited by such a curious collection of plants and animals. But it is especially a story about change.

The Galápagos hawk has no natural enemies and is the top predator on the islands. The hawks hunt young iguanas, lava lizards, land birds, seabirds, centipedes, and grasshoppers. They are also scavengers and feed on the bodies of dead animals.

The Galápagos Islands are home to the world's only marine iguanas, remarkable reptiles that bask on the rocky coast and dive offshore for seaweed, their main source of food.

The islands are named after their most famous residents, the giant tortoises. *Galápago* means "tortoise" in Spanish.

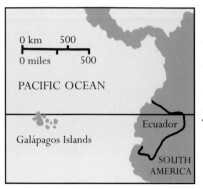

Today, there are thirteen major islands in the Galápagos chain, six smaller islands, and dozens of tiny islets. It hasn't always been this way. Over nine million years ago, hundreds of miles from the land mass now called South America, in a place that looked like any other in the expanse of ocean, an event occurred that vastly changed this once endless seascape. A volcano rose from the water, steaming and hissing, fiery and hot. When the streams of lava stopped flowing and the clouds of ash cleared and the steam blew away, a brand new island stood cooling and hardening in the cold ocean water, a bare and stony mass.

The new island was just the tip of a huge submarine mountain, the result of years and years of underwater volcanic eruptions. Each successive eruption added more lava to the top of the volcano, making it grow taller and closer to the ocean surface, until finally it burst into the air and the volcano top became an island.

On the island of Bartolomé lava once spewed into the air through small volcanic openings called vents. Over time, as the lava fell, it formed these steep-sided spatter cones encircling each opening.

PACIFIC OCEAN

Wolf

Pinta

Santiago

Bartolomé

San Cristóbal

Fernandina

Isabela

Santa
Cruz

Floreana

Española

As there are many islands, only those mentioned in the text
are labeled.

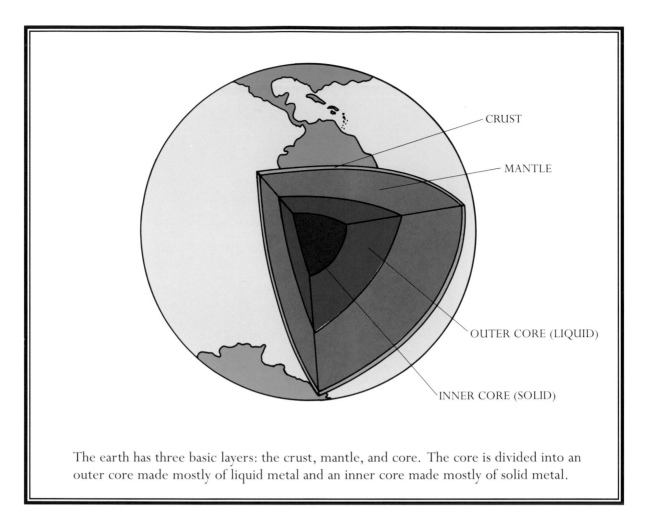

CRUST

MANTLE

OUTER CORE (LIQUID)

INNER CORE (SOLID)

The earth has three basic layers: the crust, mantle, and core. The core is divided into an outer core made mostly of liquid metal and an inner core made mostly of solid metal.

To appreciate why the island formed in that particular spot in the Pacific Ocean requires an understanding of the structure of the earth. The earth has three basic layers. At the center of the earth is the core, which is made mostly of solid metal surrounded by extremely hot, liquid metal. Above the core lies the mantle: a layer of hot, dense, rocky material. On top of the mantle lies the crust. The crust is not one unbroken layer but consists of several sections, some larger than others. The crust is similar to the shell of a hard-boiled egg cracked into about fifteen pieces. The sections of the earth's crust, called tectonic plates, are huge. A single plate can contain a whole continent. Despite their size, these plates move; they float and slide very slowly on top of the mantle at a rate of approximately two inches a year. South America, for example, travels westward on the South American plate.

The new island rose where it did because far, far below the ocean, down in the earth's mantle, is a hot spot. A hot spot is an area of intense heat rooted deep in the earth, rather like an enormous blowtorch. Scientists believe hot spots cause superheated, rocky material

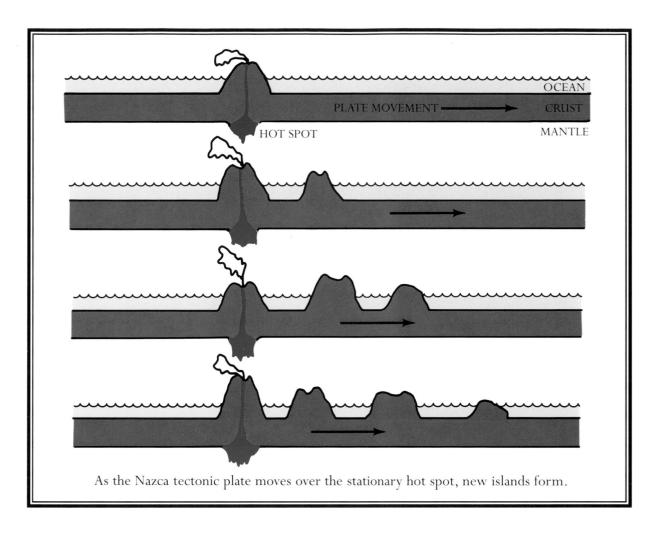

As the Nazca tectonic plate moves over the stationary hot spot, new islands form.

from near the earth's core, called magma, to rise in a column.

The fierce heat rising from a hot spot melts the overlying mantle and crust; the column of magma can then flow up through the crust to form a volcano on the earth's surface. Eventually, after many, many eruptions of hot magma, a volcanic mountain forms. Hot spots have created many of Earth's volcanoes, some on land, some in the ocean, but not all volcanoes are caused by hot spots.

The Galápagos hot spot is a crucial source of change, for it created each volcanic island, one after another, over millions of years, until a chain of islands lay strung out in the ocean. This chain was formed by the movement of the tectonic plate over the hot spot. A hot spot stays approximately in the same place, but the plate hovering over the hot spot keeps moving. The plate above the hot spot in the Galápagos, called the Nazca plate, is moving slowly to the east. Once an island arises, it is eventually carried away from the hot spot by the plate movement, like an item on a conveyor belt. Then the next island in the chain begins to form over the stationary hot spot.

The motion of the tides has carved and polished the hardened volcanic ash of this beach on Santiago.

Sometimes, if the volcanoes arise very close together, they may become part of the same island. In this way, the island Isabela came to have six volcanoes, while the other islands have only one.

Scientists believe the frequent volcanic eruptions on the western edge of the Galápagos chain mark the location of the hot spot. The age of the islands supports this belief: the westernmost islands are relatively young, no more than seven hundred thousand years old, while the easternmost islands (farthest from the estimated location of the hot spot) are about three million years old. Recent geologic studies suggest even older islands lie farther to the east—islands that are now submerged.

Each island born from the hot spot began its existence bare and exposed to the tropical sun. No plants or animals lived on the newly formed lava rocks. Waves broke on rugged, empty coasts.

Over time, volcanic eruptions followed by erosion created these dramatic, ashy landforms on the islands of Bartolomé and, across the water, Santiago.

An extraordinary type of lava called *pahoehoe* is found on this century-old lava flow on Santiago. The wrinkles are formed when the intense heat of subsurface molten lava buckles and wrinkles the overlying surface lava. *Pahoehoe*, the Hawaiian word for "ropy," also occurs in the Hawaiian island chain, which was also formed over a hot spot.

Frigate birds are excellent fliers and could have reached the Galápagos early in the islands' development, but would not have lingered long. Unlike ground-nesting birds, the frigate nests in trees. The males inflate their red neck sacs to attract a mate.

Life arrived slowly to the islands, over millions of years and in a variety of ways, gradually transforming the barren landscape. The exact story of how life first came to the islands is not known because no one was there to witness it, but through experiments and educated guesses, scientists have pieced together what possibly happened.

The first life probably arrived by air. The Galápagos lie in the path of strong prevailing winds, called trade winds, that blow from the east across North and South America. Seabirds often ride these winds and, being strong fliers, were perhaps the first to discover the new islands far from land. The distance to the islands is relatively short for true seabirds, which can fly great lengths without stopping. Waved albatrosses, for example, regularly fly more than six hundred miles from their homes on the islands to the coast of South America.

The barren islands were well suited for seabirds that nest on the ground, such as red-billed tropic birds, blue-footed boobies, and petrels. These laid their eggs on the bare stones and rocky cliffs. Although the land was desolate, the ocean was rich with an abundance of fish to eat.

A ground-nesting seabird capable of living on newly formed islands, American oystercatchers lay their eggs among the rocks just above the high-tide line. They use their long, stout bills to probe the shore for crabs and mollusks.

Blue-footed boobies (left) could survive on young islands because they do not need vegetation for food or shelter. They lay their eggs on the ground and incubate them on top of their foot webs. These birds dive for fish from heights of fifty feet or more. Air sacs in their skulls act as cushions to prevent injury when they hit the water.

Red-footed boobies (right) nest in trees and shrubs and did not live on the islands until plants began to grow.

13

The trade winds also brought the tiny beginnings of plant life. Many seeds are very small and light and can travel long distances by air. Relatives of the dandelion are common on the islands because their tufted seeds are easily swept up and carried by a wind. Many different seeds also came with the birds: carried in their stomachs, stuck to the mud on their feet, or hitchhiking as sticky burrs caught on their feathers.

At first, only plants able to grow without soil survived on the Galápagos. The small, light spores of fungi, algae, and other simple organisms took hold on the barren rock. Slowly, over thousands of years, these organisms and rain, waves, and wind broke down the rock, and soil slowly formed. A wider variety of seeds and spores could then take root, if they happened to fall in the cracks and crevices where the soil lay. Grasses, ferns, and other small plants slowly established themselves, and eventually shrubs and trees began to grow, altering the face of the islands.

Once plants began to thrive, the islands became much more habitable for animals that needed vegetation for food or for shelter from the blistering sun.

These tough tiquilia plants are early pioneers of dry, ash-covered slopes. Nectar from their flowers provides food for insects.

The trip to the Galápagos would have been hard for land birds that were too weak to fly the distance under their own power, such as finches and mockingbirds. These were probably blown to the islands on wild storm winds.

Many other small creatures also blew in with the wind. Scientists who today collect wind-borne organisms by towing nets behind airplanes have discovered spiders and other small creatures thousands of miles from their native homes. It is therefore likely that the wind swept up bees, butterflies, beetles, spiders, and even tiny land snails from the mainland and whisked them to the islands.

The islands were changed not only by animals and plants arriving by wind but also by life-forms that came by sea. They were carried by currents that run like rivers through the ocean. The Humboldt Current begins in Antarctica and flows north along the Pacific coast of South America until, south of the equator, it heads west, straight for the Galápagos.

The buoyant seeds of beach-loving plants such as mangroves, saltbushes, and sea grapes floating on the Humboldt Current would have washed up on shore and taken

1.

2.

3.

1. Islands rising from the hot spot created new shallow water environments that provide homes to many plants and animals such as the spotted eagle ray.

2. Among the fish that scour rocks and crevices for food are white banded angelfish.

3. Sally Lightfoot crabs begin their lives as tiny, free-swimming larvae that may be carried long distances on ocean currents, which may be how crabs first came to the Galápagos.

4. Galápagos fur seals are not seals at all. Because they have visible ears and use their front flippers to swim, they are considered a type of sea lion.

5. Pacific green turtles venture onto land to lay their eggs at night. Scientists know little of where sea turtles go in their ocean wanderings, but recent studies suggest they may travel long migratory routes that follow the hills and valleys of the ocean floor.

root. Fur seals, sea lions, and penguins—all excellent swimmers—may have made the long journey to the islands following schools of fish. Marine turtles most likely discovered the islands during their oceanic wanderings. These turtles often embark on long trips: Pacific green turtles tagged near their nests in the Galápagos have been found off the coasts of Ecuador and Costa Rica.

Scientists propose that giant tortoises and other animals that could not swim or fly were trapped on logs or hunks of vegetation torn from the mainland during floods and storms and carried to the Galápagos on the strong ocean currents. Iguanas, geckos, snakes, ants, and scorpions, among others, probably arrived by means of these floating tangles of plants and debris.

The landing of these natural rafts was a rare and haphazard event. A raft washed to sea must drift through miles and miles of open ocean before bumping by chance into the Galápagos. Hundreds of years can pass between landings. Also, rafts may reach islands not suitable for the rafters: islands without food plants such as cacti or tomatoes would not support tortoises; snakes would die on an island without rats or other creatures to eat.

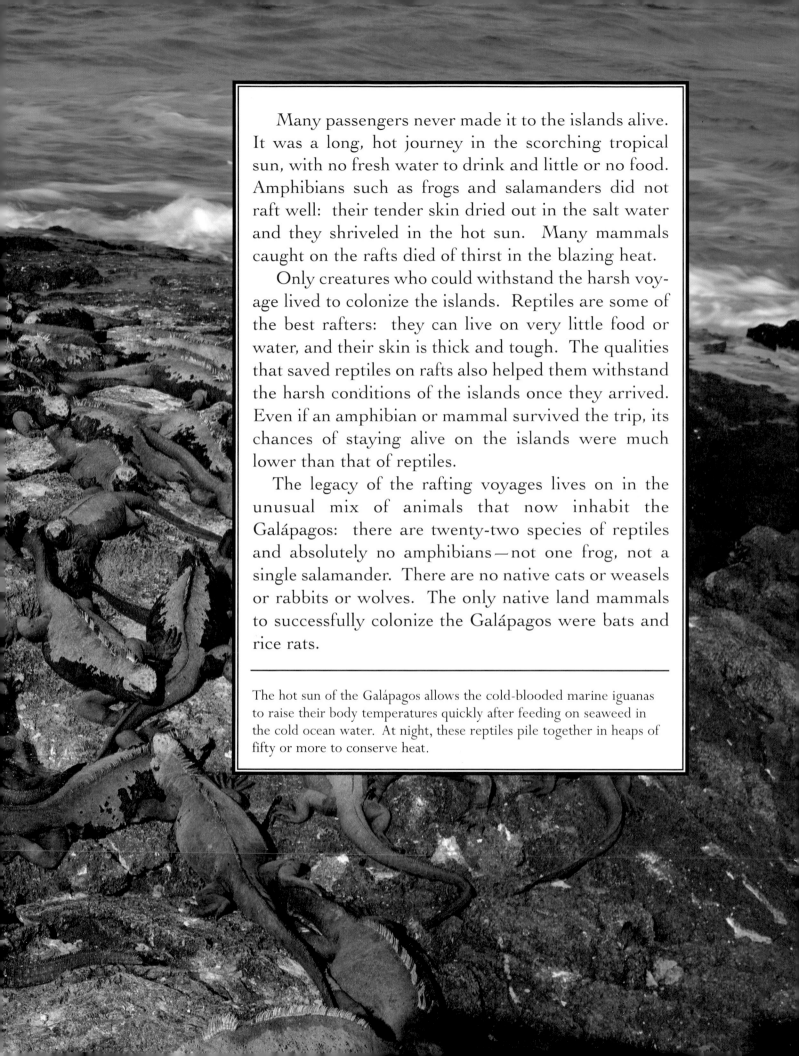

Many passengers never made it to the islands alive. It was a long, hot journey in the scorching tropical sun, with no fresh water to drink and little or no food. Amphibians such as frogs and salamanders did not raft well: their tender skin dried out in the salt water and they shriveled in the hot sun. Many mammals caught on the rafts died of thirst in the blazing heat.

Only creatures who could withstand the harsh voyage lived to colonize the islands. Reptiles are some of the best rafters: they can live on very little food or water, and their skin is thick and tough. The qualities that saved reptiles on rafts also helped them withstand the harsh conditions of the islands once they arrived. Even if an amphibian or mammal survived the trip, its chances of staying alive on the islands were much lower than that of reptiles.

The legacy of the rafting voyages lives on in the unusual mix of animals that now inhabit the Galápagos: there are twenty-two species of reptiles and absolutely no amphibians—not one frog, not a single salamander. There are no native cats or weasels or rabbits or wolves. The only native land mammals to successfully colonize the Galápagos were bats and rice rats.

The hot sun of the Galápagos allows the cold-blooded marine iguanas to raise their body temperatures quickly after feeding on seaweed in the cold ocean water. At night, these reptiles pile together in heaps of fifty or more to conserve heat.

Well suited to dry places, lichens can grow without soil and are often found clinging to trees, rocks, and even the shells of giant tortoises.

Sea lions find a comfortable place to relax on this rock formation made of hardened ash on Santiago.

And so, over millions of years, a web of life grew, transforming the Galápagos from a chain of bare rocks into a variety of landscapes.

This green field covered with ferns and grasses on Santa Cruz was once a barren, volcanic crater.

Opuntia cacti stand above sea lions. Opuntia species play a vital role in the dry Galápagos lowlands. Their fruit, flowers, seeds, and pulpy pads feed giant tortoises, land iguanas, doves, mockingbirds, two species of cactus finches, and weevils. Cactus finches peck the pads for water.

Well equipped for ocean life, marine iguanas can stay underwater for an hour. They remove excess salt ingested with their seaweed diet via specialized glands that open into their nostrils. Frequent sneezing expels salt, which coats their heads with a white crust.

When plants and animals reached the islands, they faced new environments and new challenges. Some species died out because the challenges were too great. Other species over time adapted to their new surroundings.

The mystery of these adaptations was studied by the biologist Charles Darwin, who sailed to the Galápagos aboard HMS *Beagle* in 1835. He observed marine iguanas, which swim in the ocean to feed on seaweed and are the only sea-swimming lizards in the world. He witnessed sunflowers that grew as tall as trees, and giant tortoises that weighed over six hundred pounds. Although it was his only visit and he stayed just five weeks, the observations Darwin made in the Galápagos raised questions he spent the remainder of his life trying to answer.

No group changed more dramatically in the Galápagos than plants in the sunflower family. Some sunflower relatives are trees (left) that can reach more than forty feet high, while others grow no larger than small shrubs (right). Twenty types of sunflower relatives live on the islands today, all descendants of a single type that arrived in the Galápagos long ago.

Land iguanas thrive in dry landscapes away from shore. They obtain most of their water from eating cacti and other plants. The color of adult males can grow much brighter when they fight other males for territory.

How did life in the Galápagos become so unique and so variable? Darwin sensed that life on the islands became different through one of nature's most hidden and powerful forces of change: evolution. He argued that all species evolve, or change slowly over time. In 1858, Darwin presented his theory of evolution in London along with another great naturalist, Alfred Russel Wallace, who independently had come up with similar ideas.

Opuntia cacti, distinguished by their flat pads, grow here among candelabra cacti. Like the sunflower relatives, opuntia evolved into many types on the islands, including sprawling, shrubby, and treelike forms. The treelike opuntia has pads high on its trunk (such as those pictured here), a possible defense against land iguanas and giant tortoises, which love to eat them.

Evolution explains why ten different races of tortoise inhabit the Galápagos. Biologists believe that long ago only one race of tortoise lived on the islands. These founding tortoises all looked more or less the same; then the race evolved in different directions due to the unique environments of each island.

Here is one way this change could have come about according to the theory of evolution: Some of the early tortoises arrived on low, dry islands where few plants grew. Food was hard to find. Tortoises that by chance had longer necks survived more often because they could reach high up on plants to eat fruit and leaves other tortoises could not reach. Longer-necked tortoises with shells curved like a saddle could stretch their necks even higher. These tortoises were more apt to survive and raise young. Their offspring inherited long necks and saddle-shaped shells. After many generations, only long-necked, saddle-shelled tortoises remained.

Other early tortoises landed on islands with lush hillsides, where plants were abundant. The tortoises on these islands did not need long necks to reach food. A shell curved like a saddle also was not necessary. Tortoises with shells shaped more like a large dome actually did better, perhaps because domes provide more protection than saddles when pushing through dense undergrowth. On these islands tortoises evolved short necks and domed shells.

The type of evolution that occurs when certain characteristics (such as long necks or saddle-shaped shells) are favored because they help individuals survive and reproduce is called natural selection. Other types of evolutionary change occur, but it is mostly through natural selection that plants and animals become better adapted to their environment.

Tortoises with dome-shaped shells (bottom) fight less often than tortoises with saddle-shaped shells (top). Not only are saddle-shaped shells useful for reaching high up on plants for food, they also help tortoises in battles against each other for scarce resources and mates. Tortoises use their heads to butt each other, so those with the longest necks usually win.

The Galápagos finches provide another example of natural selection. Thirteen finch species inhabit the Galápagos. Some finches eat ticks and mites from the hides of tortoises and iguanas. Other finches eat seeds. There are even finches on Wolf Island that drink the blood of red-footed and masked boobies. Each finch species has a uniquely shaped beak that suits its particular diet.

The thirteen finch species are all descendants from a single early species that arrived on the islands long ago. Biologists believe that, because finches are seedeaters almost everywhere else, the first Galápagos finches all ate seeds. But many of the birds were forced to adopt new ways of life on the islands because seeds were scarce and competition was often intense. Some finches tried to eat insects while others tried to eat leaves. At first these attempts may not have been very successful. Only finches with beak shapes or other characteristics suitable for their new diet thrived. The offspring of surviving finches inherited their parents' beak shape and fed as their parents had fed. Generation after generation, natural selection caused the finches to change.

The first finches to arrive on the islands looked more or less the same, but they evolved over time into many new species, each species with a characteristic beak shape specialized to a particular diet. The skull and its muscular structure evolved with the beak, enabling the bird to utilize the beak as a specialized tool to obtain food. For instance, tree finches apply pressure at the tip of their beaks, which helps them to grasp and tear away wood in search of insects. Ground finches apply pressure at the base of their beaks, which helps them to crush hard-shelled seeds. The vegetarian finch is unusual because it can use its beak to both crush and grasp. It eats mostly fruits, buds, and leaves.

WARBLER FINCH

Finches with pointed beaks can probe trees, cacti, flowers, and other plants for insects or nectar.

MEDIUM TREE FINCH

Finches with grasping beaks can dig insects out of wood.

LARGE GROUND FINCH

Finches with thick, heavy beaks can crack large seeds.

Scientists believe the first cormorants to colonize the islands could fly, but because there were no predators on land, flying was not essential. With an abundant food supply just off-shore, diving was more important. Over time, cormorant wings became progressively smaller and weaker.

When natural selection causes a particular plant or animal population faced with many new environments to evolve into many new races or species, the process is called adaptive radiation. Adaptive radiation is especially common on islands, because islands are isolated and each has its own unique set of environments. Populations, such as the first finches, that find themselves on different islands often evolve in different directions.

This does not mean natural selection on islands always causes one species to diverge into many; sometimes change occurs in only one direction. Galápagos cormorants are a good example. These birds evolved into excellent divers on the islands, but in so doing lost their ability to fly. Galápagos cormorants underwent a remarkable transformation, but this did not lead to many new species: only one species of cormorant inhabits all the Galápagos Islands today, and it is flightless.

Evolution is difficult to observe but not impossible. In 1977, the biologists Peter and Rosemary Grant discovered that a single drought caused evolutionary change in Galápagos ground finches. Small seeds became scarce during the drought. Many smaller finches that depended on these seeds did not survive. Large finches with big beaks did better (because they could eat larger seeds) and passed this successful characteristic to their chicks. Although it would take more than one drought to create a whole new species of finch, this study demonstrates that evolution is ongoing and that change can happen remarkably fast.

Today's cormorants are earthbound. They share the land and water with another flightless bird, the Galápagos penguin, which lost its ability to fly long before it reached the islands. Of all the cormorants in the world, only the Galápagos cormorants are flightless.

under the oceans. The crust is the least dense layer of the earth. *See also* **Soil**.

Evolution. The theory proposed independently by Charles Darwin and Alfred Wallace explaining how species change over time.

— **Adaptive radiation.** A phenomenon by which a single group of similar organisms encounters a variety of new habitats and evolves into many different types. Finches, tortoises, and plants in the sunflower family underwent adaptive radiation in the Galápagos. In each case, a single group evolved into many different types in response to the different environments on the islands.

— **Natural selection.** The process by which a population changes because some individuals possess traits that allow them to survive and reproduce better than other individuals. Over time, the population becomes better adapted to its environment because successful traits are inherited more often than traits that are not successful.

Erosion. The process by which rocks and soil are broken down and worn away by running water, ice, wind, or waves.

Seamount. The seamounts of the Galápagos are sunken islands, but not all seamounts form in this way. *Seamount* is a general term for a submarine mountain rising a thousand meters or higher above the ocean floor, sometimes occurring singly, sometimes occurring in a chain.

Soil. The thin, uppermost layer of the earth's crust made of rock fragments, clay, minerals, and organic matter such as decomposed plants and animals. Most land plants need soil to grow. *See also* **crust**, *under* **Earth structure**.

Tectonic plates. The crust is broken into about fifteen major tectonic plates that move or slide slowly over the earth's mantle. Plates move in different directions and can collide with one another, sometimes causing intense volcanic activity and mountain formation. The Andes mountains were created when the Nazca plate (moving east) collided with the South American plate (moving west).

Trade winds are strong, major wind systems that blow almost constantly in one direction. One system (the Northeast trade winds) starts in the Northern Hemisphere and blows down toward the equator. The other system (the Southeast trade winds) starts in the Southern Hemisphere and blows up toward the equator. Both of these trade winds blow across the Galápagos.

Volcano. A vent in the earth's crust through which molten rock, gases, and ash erupt. *Volcano* also refers to the mountain built up around the vent by ejected material. Volcanoes usually form at the boundaries of tectonic plates. Volcanoes formed by hot spots, such as volcanoes of the Galápagos and Hawaii, are unusual in that they were formed within a tectonic plate, not along its edge.

— **Magma.** Rock liquefied by heat below the earth's surface. When magma reaches the surface of the earth, it is called **lava**.

— **Hot spot.** An area of intense heat a few hundred miles across, originating deep in the mantle. Magma rising in the hot spot causes volcanic activity on the earth's surface.

For Mickey Born Myers
—L. B. M. and C. A. M.

For Esmé and Ruth
—N. F.

PHOTOGRAPHER'S NOTE

The Galápagos Islands are famous for their profusion of diverse and unique creatures. Through research and speculation based on this life, we have learned much about evolution. I journeyed to the islands, however, to photograph the land itself, to discover what it had to offer. I was fully rewarded by what I found.

The islands vary in age and are at different stages in their development. Even in the minuscule amount of time that we are allowed to observe the events of the islands, we may in fact witness much, as well as study the results of changes that occurred before. Calderas collapse. Beaches are swept into the sea. Each incident is a part of the geological evolutionary process of birth, aging, and death.

By documenting with my camera this diverse landscape, I believe that I have been able to contribute to the understanding that the land, too, has a cycle of life.

—N. F.

ACKNOWLEDGMENTS
The authors thank the Charles Darwin Foundation, Inc.,
Dr. D. M. Christie, Dr. Thomas Fritts, Dr. Dennis Geist, Dr. Rosemary Grant,
and the folks at the Charles Darwin Research Station, all of whom provided valuable comments.

The publisher wishes to thank Johanna Barry and Susana Struve
at the Charles Darwin Foundation, Inc. for their assistance.

FIRST EDITION
1 3 5 7 9 10 8 6 4 2

Myers, Christopher A.
Galápagos: islands of change/Christopher and Lynne Myers; photographs by Nathan Farb.—1st ed.
p. cm.
ISBN 0-7868-0074-7—ISBN 0-7868-2061-6 (lib. bdg.)
1. Natural history—Galápagos Islands—Juvenile literature.
2. Galápagos Islands—Juvenile literature.
[1. Natural history-Galápagos Islands. 2. Galápagos Islands.]
I. Myers, Lynne Born.
II. Farb, Nathan, 1941- ill. III. Title.
QH198. G3M94 1995
508.866'5—dc20
94-26173 CIP AC